FORGET FORECLOSURES

BUY HOUSES *from* DEAD PEOPLE

a complete and invaluable guide including true-life stories.

ARLEEN RICE

ISBN: 1-4392-6465-1
ISBN-13: 9781439264652

DEDICATION

To my daughter, Laura.
She always said,
"Go big…or go home!"
I dedicate this book to her.

ACKNOWLEDGEMENTS

Thanks to all my friends, family and loved ones for their help and support in writing this book. A special thanks to my friend Leanne Hoagland-Smith for her expertise, advice and constant encouragement. She pushed me to "Get it done!"

TABLE OF CONTENTS

INTRODUCTION IX

MY PERSONAL STORY 1

SIX DISADVANTAGES OF BUYING FORECLOSURES 15

FIVE ADVANTAGES OF "BUYING HOUSES FROM DEAD PEOPLE" . . .23

CHOOSING A NEIGHBORHOOD 29

KNOWING NEIGHBORHOOD PROPERTY VALUES 35

EVALUATING YOUR ABILITIES 41

EVALUATING YOUR ABILITIES WORKSHEETS 45

KNOWING YOUR COSTS 55

ASSEMBLING YOUR TEAM 59

LOCATING AVAILABLE PROPERTIES 65

WRITING THE LETTER 73

ASSESSING THE CONDITION 77

ASSESSING THE CONDITION WORKSHEETS 81

MAKING AN OFFER 119

CLOSING THE DEAL 123

REVIEW: ARE YOU READY? 127

INTRODUCTION

"If you want to be successful, find someone who has achieved the results you want and copy what they do and you'll achieve the same results."

Tony Robbins

Let's be honest. There are some individuals who believe that "Buy Houses From Dead People" is a guide preparing you to prey upon and take advantage of the elderly or the family members of the recently departed.

However, a few others may believe that "Buy Houses From Dead People" is a guide on how to create a circumstance that benefits two parties while providing a service.

"Buy Houses From Dead People" is in fact a guide designed to change your mindset from obtaining the home of your dreams or getting rich by purchasing real estate through foreclosures, to seeking out higher quality properties from the elderly or the recently departed who are no longer in need of their homes.

Elderly people in their eighties and nineties are dying or moving in with relatives. Some may be moving into assisted living or nursing homes leaving their children, who may be in their sixties or seventies, with the responsibility of selling their home.

The purpose of this light-hearted guide is to persuade you by contrasting the disadvantages of buying foreclosures, to the benefits and advantages of purchasing properties from the elderly or the recently departed for as low as 65% of their current market value.

Throughout this guide, you will read specific facts supporting this purpose.

This guide enables you to contrast the:
- Disadvantages of buying foreclosures
- Advantages of buying homes from the recently departed or from the elderly in transition

Next you will learn the importance of:
- Choosing the most profitable neighborhoods
- Researching the current market value of the homes in those areas
- Evaluating your abilities
- Knowing labor and material costs

"Buy Houses From Dead People" will:
- Help you assemble a fail-safe team
- Aid you in increasing your potential profits
- Provide you with a checklist ensuring that you are prepared to take the next steps

Also, you will discover how to:
- Locate available or soon to be available properties
- Approach neighbors
- Talk to acquaintances
- Analyze an obituary
- Write an effective introduction letter

Lastly, this invaluable guide will assist you in:
- Assessing the real estate's condition
- Pricing the amount on your "Offer to Purchase" agreement based on knowledge
- Creating a contract
- Presenting the offer
- Closing the deal

This guide has it all! Everything you need to secure the skill of purchasing available, or soon to be available, properties from the elderly or the recently departed at bargain prices.

And remember, by using the techniques in "Buy Houses From Dead People," you are "creating an opportunity that benefits two parties while providing a service."

"Knowledge is of two kinds.
We know a subject ourselves, or
we know where we can find information upon it."

Samuel Johnson

MY PERSONAL STORY

"Always bear in mind that your own resolution to succeed is more important than any other."

Abraham Lincoln

There I was…divorced with an eleven year old daughter, no cash, $7,000 in consumer debt, a stack of cancelled credit cards and the burden of two completely mortgaged rental properties. (One I bought from a dead person.) I needed a plan.

First, I moved into the smaller rental property. This house had been a rental for over 6 years and was looking a little shabby. After I stopped crying and feeling sorry for myself, I pulled up my sleeves and went to work.

I painted everything inside and out. On the floor, I installed oak parquet flooring in the kitchen, laundry room and foyer, vinyl in the bathroom and carpeted the rest. Next, I replaced the kitchen countertops, faucet and cabinet hardware. For a final touch, I replaced the front storm door, old shutters and landscaped the front yard.

Now the view from the curb was no longer shabby, but warm and inviting.

I placed a <u>For Sale</u> sign in the front yard along with an ad in the local newspaper under "Houses for Sale." Less than thirty days later the house was "SOLD." My down payment of twenty percent of the original purchased price, plus two thousand dollars I had spent updating the house, resulted in an approximate 187% return on my investment!

With momentum building, I put the second rental property up for sale, "as is." I purchased this property (for a very reasonable amount) from the estate of the little old lady who lived across the street from my parents. The lady and her husband never had any children or pets and had always kept the house in excellent condition.

The house was painted white inside and out. The hardwood floors were covered with avocado green sculptured carpet. All the original, natural oak woodwork was stunning and in excellent condition. The landscaping was a little overgrown but had always been well manicured.

Again, I repeated the same sale process. A <u>For Sale</u> sign placed in the front yard and an ad in the local newspaper. And again, in one month, the house was "SOLD." An approximate 97% return on my twenty percent down payment of the original purchased price.

I was on a roll and ready for another project. Everyday I would pass this small quaint Cape Cod home my way to work. The house looked a little tired and for some reason I wrote the following letter and mailed it to the address:

Dear Sir or Madam,

I drive past your house everyday on my way to work and think that it would be a perfect home for my daughter and me.

If you are ever interested in selling it, please contact me at 555-XXXX.

Regards,
Arleen Rice

One week later, I received a phone call. The owner said that they were going to sell their house. She had a death in her family and inherited a little money. She and her husband had purchased a new home. They had been doing a little redecorating before they moved in and just had not had the time to put their house up for sale. We made an agreement, hired an attorney to write it up and within a month my daughter and I were in.

Once in, with the help of friends, I painted and wallpapered the entire interior, removed the beige sculptured carpeting, sanded and refinished the hardwood floors, painted the exterior, installed new shutters and replaced the landscaping.

I loved this house. It was perfect for my daughter and me. In less than three months, I had redecorated and sold two rental properties and upgraded to a nicer home.

Of course, there is no gain without pain. That summer I had foot surgery. As I passed the days reading and recuperating with my foot elevated on the front porch, I noticed a lot of traffic happening to the house next door. The owner had died and the house was empty. From where I was sitting, all I saw was gallons of white paint going in and yards of old carpeting going out. Even though I could not see the style or color of the carpeting, I was sure it had to be sculptured and avocado green! Contractors had been going in and out of the house for weeks. I asked them what they were doing. "Just a little clean up!" was their reply. Something inside of me told me that I had to see the interior of this house. My curiosity peaked. I persisted in asking to see it. Finally, I was in.

Apparently, the old gentleman had a few "accidents" during the last few weeks of his life. There were two "accidents" in his bedroom, one in the den and two in the living room. I know it sounds bad…but it wasn't.

The house was so similar to mine, but a little larger and nicer. I learned this house had been built by the same builder. Now I just had to have it. So once again, with paper in hand, I wrote this letter and sent it to the address:

Dear Sir or Madam,

It is my understanding that this house may be for sale.

I would be interested in purchasing it as is. You can contact me at 555-XXXX.

Regards,
Arleen Rice

This time I was not surprised that I received a call. In the conversation I expressed my love for this house and that I really wanted to purchase it "as is." The deceased owner's daughter was a successful attorney who wanted to rid herself of the ongoing hassle of the repair work. We made an agreement, drew up legal documents and within a month it was mine!

Now, I had to sell my house that I was living in. Since it looked great…freshly painted, landscaped and all, I placed my For Sale sign in the front yard and put an ad in the local newspaper.

As always, I listed the address and the asking price of this property. Buyers would know if the house was in their price range and knowing the address they could drive buy to see if they liked it before they called. I didn't want phone calls…I wanted prospective buyers.

Again, within a month I had an agreement. My attorney drew up a contract and the house was "SOLD." An approximate 137% return in four months on my investment of a down payment and redecorating costs.

Hey, this was starting to be a lot of fun. Plus it was profitable! I called my moving company (they were beginning to become my friends) and told them "I needed two guys and no truck." I was literally moving twenty-five feet to the house next door!

The old story repeated itself with overgrown landscaping, white paint and unfinished floors. My hardwood floor guy had to replace some of the damaged flooring before refinishing. He did a great job. You could not see the repairs he had made.

Becoming quite the professional painter, I painted everything inside and out. I also designed and replaced the old landscaping.

The house had an excellent floor plan with several built-ins, great fireplace and solid bones. It was a true classic.

The kitchen was small and outdated. I felt a remodel would be worth the cost because of course, I was going to stay and live in this house. My family and friends were done giving up their weekends and free labor. A contractor was needed. I found a maintenance man doing "side work" to perform the remodeling. He removed the kitchen wall, opening the space into the dining room. What an improvement that was!

With a little drywall, new cherry cabinets, counters, flooring, appliances, a fresh coat of paint inside and out, a little landscaping and presto…the house was beautiful! A lady in her car stopped and told me "You are improving our neighborhood!" and thanked me. Oh yes, I failed to mention that now I believed I was an impressive decorator and a fairly skillful landscaper.

A couple of winters came and went. One day I was driving by an open house on a nearby lake. I got out of my car as the realtor was locking up. "Oh, come on in." he said. I told him I was just driving around and basically "Just killing time." He asked me to "Please come in." It had been a slow day and he wanted me to sign the guest book.

The kitchen looked as if someone had made coffee, ate a light breakfast and left. I asked him "Did someone die?" He said "No." The elderly lady that owned the house had fallen and went to a nursing home. I looked at the price on the sell sheet and left.

Later, I told a friend about that house for sale on the lake. He told me something that I do not know to be true, but that I will never forget. "You know," he said, "I believe it is a fact that if you offer forty people 50% less than their asking price, one out of the forty will accept it." I didn't believe it.

The next day I walked into the realtor's office. I offered 66% of the asking price. He said the seller was in Florida and that I would have to wait seventy-two hours for a reply. I waited patiently. The next day, the realtor presented me with the sellers counter at 78% of their asking price.

Wow! I had to go back and look at the place since I was only in this house for less than ten minutes. The house was better than I had remembered. Hardwood floors were under the yes…avocado green sculptured carpet. It had a new high-end furnace and a newly sheeted and shingled roof. I was excited. Really excited!

I returned with the intention of a compromised offer of 70% of the original asking price. However, when I entered the realtor's office I told him that their counter offer was acceptable. The house was clearly worth it. But I explained to the realtor that I could only afford my original offer of 66% of the asking price. I would have to wait and if the owners could not find a buyer at a later date, I would extend my offer.

Handing him my banker's business card, I told the realtor he could call her. If and when the sellers changed their minds, my banker would confirm that I could close on the property (and the sellers would receive their money) in two weeks or as long as it took to process the paperwork, proving a quick sale. Little did I know that a two week closing date was the key to closing the deal.

The very next day, the realtor called me and said the sellers had accepted my offer.

What I learned was the woman who owned the house was in her nineties. She had only one child, a seventy year old daughter living in Florida. The daughter was remodeling her condo with plans to accommodate her mother. The cost of the remodeling was exactly what I had offered. Winter was coming and it seems she did not want to take care of the lake house during the winter. She also had to drive from Florida to the Midwest to get her mother out of the nursing home. These facts, unknown to me, had influenced her decision. Two weeks later we closed.

Out came the For Sale sign again for the house I was living in. It sold in less than forty-five days. I had invested about $10,000 into the updating, adding to my twenty percent down payment. I closed in less than forty-five days for an approximate 129% return on my investment. I was off to the lake.

This time I hired a decorator to pick out paint and wallpaper. Talk about taking it to the next level! She made me realize that I was good at decorating a room or two, but her expertise made the entire house flow. The house had this warm and cozy cottage feel to it with a great fireplace.

Two years later, with a little yard work, new storm door, new kitchen countertops and faucet, refinished hardwood floors and a remodeled bathroom, I sold this house too. I had invested an additional $10,000 and in the end it paid off. I sold it for a 66% gain. That equaled an approximate 222% return on my original investment of a twenty percent down payment and the cost of the redecorating/remodeling.

Across the lake from my "SOLD" cottage, an elderly lady had recently died leaving her son with the task of selling her home. Her son told me that he had mowed her lawn for "forty years." This information indicated to me that she owned the house for decades. (And yes, I have to say this… it too had avocado green sculptured carpeting!) Presuming the property was free and clear of any mortgages, I offered to buy her house "as is" for 81% of the asking price. Though I asked for sixty days to close, I also asked the seller to include the tractor/mower in the shed. Again, I offered my banker's business card and said she would confirm that my financing was pre-approved.

The seller accepted my offer. I still own this lake house today and use it as a cottage. Oh yes, and it is now worth about 230% of what I paid for it.

By now you may be thinking that I prey on the elderly, or that I take advantage of families in their time of grief. Don't believe it!

I create an opportunity that benefits two parties while providing a needed service. First of all, the deceased are generally family members who were very old. Old people are expected to die because death is a part of the life cycle.

The deceased houses are often dated, in need of upgrading and definitely redecorating. By buying and improving these houses the neighboring properties also increase in value.

So again, I am providing a service and a fast and easy way for inconvenienced people to unload a burden. Don't see it that way?

- Who is going to pay the taxes?
- Who is going to pay the utility bills?
- Who is going to mow the lawn, clean gutters, rake leaves and plow the snow?

An empty house deteriorates fast. Now do you get the picture?

Here is another true story. My mother returned home from a bus trip to Branson, Missouri. "You're not going to believe this…but in the middle of lunch, on the bus, a man died!" she said. "Really?!" "Where did he live?" I asked…and I bought his house.

I made an offer to purchase his house "as is," for 57% of the family's original asking price. My offer was refused.

The family kept it on the market. Months passed. They paid the taxes, utilities, kept up the lawn, painted the entire interior and replaced the furnace. Still there were no acceptable offers to purchase the house. I bought it almost a year later for approximately 68% of the original asking price.

It was a solid house, with an exterior of Indiana limestone. I thought I would move in, but life truly offers endless opportunities.

The day of closing, I found another house built by the same builder. This house was brick, not limestone and larger, with a bigger garage and additional bathrooms. I realized that it was a better home for me.

The owner was a man in his nineties who at the time of his death was in a nursing home. His seventy-some year old only daughter had been maintaining the house for over two years. When her father passed she wanted to sell the house quickly. She did not want to start the boiler for the winter or take care of the yard another day.

I purchased the house for approximately 68% of what the house was worth. I still live there today.

I want to tell you one last story. One day, I was reading the local paper and saw in the obituaries that an elderly lady had died whose home was in a neighborhood where I always wanted to live. I jumped in my car and drove by. A security company was installing a system. The house from the outside was exactly what I wanted. I immediately returned home and wrote this letter.

Dear Sir or Madam,

It is my understanding that this house may be for sale. I would be interested in buying it as is.

Please contact me at 555-XXXX.

Regards,
Arleen Rice
(My address)

Now this was the grandmother of a very prominent local family. "Had I become an ambulance chaser?" I wondered. I put a stamp on the letter and left it on my desk. A few days later, I dropped the letter in my desk drawer. After all, I saw members of this family several times a month having lunch and I would eventually just ask them about their grandmother's house. A couple of months passed. I saw them, but I never asked. I guess I was embarrassed.

Six months passed and I ran into an old friend. I asked about his son who had just graduated from college. "He just bought a house. He wasn't really ready for homeownership, but it was a friend's grandmother's house that was very dated inside. The price was so good we couldn't pass it up! When we walked inside, we actually made a comment that this looked like a house you would buy!" (No, this house did not have avocado green sculptured carpet. Grandma was more up-to-date than that. The carpet was two inch shag!)

Yes, it was THE house! I let it slip right through my fingers because I allowed fear to keep me from taking action. It still hurts me to say it. I hate to think about it. The stamped letter stayed in my desk drawer for months. I kept it there for a long time to remind me of the missed opportunity and not to let fear drive my actions.

In closing, I have been successful. From those successes I have integrated my experiences into a proven system. Use this system correctly and diligently and you can buy your first home, upgrade from your current home or use it to gain profits.

You will see in the next few chapters how and why this system works and why this approach is better than buying foreclosures. And remember..." You are creating an opportunity that benefits two parties while providing a needed service."

SIX DISADVANTAGES
OF BUYING FORECLOSURES

"I don't jump over 7-foot bars:
I look around for 1-foot bars I can step over."

Warren Buffet

I am relatively sure that you have purchased books seeking information on foreclosures if you have purchased this material. Foreclosures are a real buzz in the air.

- Get rich quick is the premise.
- Easy and simple.
- Someone lost their house to the bank and you can buy it cheap!

I believe some people do buy foreclosures cheap, but they are seasoned and connected. They have the inside track. These people know the bankers, lenders and realtors because they **are** the bankers, lenders and realtors…or their friends. They are experienced professionals who have been doing it for a long time.

I'm not saying you can't get "in." But why go through all that hard work and frustration only to be faced with a long list of other issues?

This chapter is all about convincing you why learning and using the techniques in "Buy Houses From Dead People" is the better alternative to buying houses in foreclosure.

DISADVANTAGE #1 - CONDITION

Let's talk about condition. I have a friend who has been a successful realtor for over 18 years. She talks about the horrible condition issues of the current foreclosures. Some of these properties are trashed! I don't mean they have trash in them. I mean that they are destroyed!

Before being evicted, the owners removed everything you can think of; light fixtures, air conditioning units, furnaces, hot water heaters, vanities, kitchen cabinets, built-in dishwashers, carpeting and anything else they could sell. Then there is the aluminum storm door and storm windows… big bucks for aluminum scrap. Does (I mean, Did) the house have aluminum siding? At least as high as a ladder will go, that siding will be gone!

I'll bet you are thinking that I have painted a pretty exaggerated picture. Okay. So let's paint a less exaggerated one. The homeowners were not vandals, just good folks who could no longer afford their home. Think about it. If they could not afford their mortgage, they surely could not afford the cost of maintaining their home in good working condition. For the past year or so, all they were doing was trying to keep their heads above water. Do you think they would give up their one night out a week and instead spend their money to fertilize their lawn, replace that broken window or replace that leaking hot water heater? Probably, not a chance!

DISADVANTAGE # 2 - VANDALISM

I agree, maybe I was a little carried away above. But I was trying to make a point. In a perfect world, the bank fore-closed on a well maintained home where the family dem-onstrated their pride. The home was in excellent condition and in working order when the homeowners left…but then what happened?

The vandals in the darkness of night crawled in like rats on a dead carcass. It was the vandals, not the good family with all that pride, who stripped the house of anything and all that could be used or sold to their advantage. People are surviving on this stuff because they are the true evil of so-ciety. You can fence it, board it up and they are still going to get in. Scavengers!

DISADVANTAGE #3 - "INSIDERS"

"Insiders" have a vantage point to a favorable position or inside knowledge. They know the details of:
- Who is in threat of foreclosure
- Where the properties are located
- Who holds the mortgage
- Amount owed on the mortgage
- Amount of time the owner has to make the mortgage "current"
- Foreclosure deadline

Truthfully, I don't know much about "insiders." What I do know is that they are out there and I am not one of them. Bankers, lawyers, realtors and their friends are "insiders." The owners and employees of businesses like insurance companies and title companies are "insiders." Don't forget the people who serve the foreclosure papers to the homeowner who has defaulted. All of these people are at the top of the buying foreclosure's list. You are at the bottom of it. And the bottom is not a good place to be.

All the good properties are quickly gone leaving you with dozens of bad properties to pursue, using your time and energy. If you cannot move up the food chain and become an "insider," buying foreclosures could be a long and painful learning experience.

DISADVANTAGE #4 - BID PROCESS

When it comes to organizing the foreclosure bidding process, every institution does them differently. Unless you work with only one mortgage institution, you will have to learn many processes. Just one mistake may disqualify your bid.

First, you will have to locate the time and place of a public sale. This can be done by checking the ads in the local newspaper, contacting the Sheriff's Department or contacting the mortgage company's attorney. The courthouse should also have a schedule of foreclosure auctions.

Next, you will need cash. Yes, I said "cash!" Most lenders will not accept any other terms. So you will need to come prepared to pay cash on the spot.

Knowing the condition of the property is of upmost importance. Unlike buying any property "as is," make sure you have evaluated its condition.

You can also contact the following federal government agencies that offer foreclosed properties:
- Treasury Department
- Internal Revenue Service
- County Real Estate Tax Sales
- Government Services Administration
- Federal Deposit Insurance Corporation

I thought buying foreclosures is supposed to be an easy way to get rich quick. By the time the house gets to this, all the good stuff is probably gone. If an acceptable property does emerge, imagine how many people you will be bidding against.

Too many emotions are involved. You've got to beat the other guy. This becomes a real competition. If you are like most people, you hate to lose...and often you will. Who wants that?

Remember, your goal is to find a quality property to fix up and resell or occupy in the quickest and easiest manner possible.

DISADVANTAGE # 5 - FINANCING

As stated previously, the terms of a public sale require that you have arranged financing ahead of time and have "cash" on hand that day. As the saying goes in this business "Cash is king!" and there are plenty of people with cash that you will be bidding against.

If you do not have cash, you will have to go to the bank and secure a short term loan or borrow from a private lender. You will be able to secure a new mortgage after you make the repairs.

DISADVANTAGE #6 - LIENS, DELINQUENT TAXES AND SECOND MORTGAGES

Most homeowners experiencing foreclosure are financially over extended. Therefore, the property may be tangled with liens, delinquent taxes and/or second mortgages. Where does the money come from to settle these burdens? Will the resolution of these complications stall your purchase of the house? Do you want to pay additional legal fees to straighten it all out?

You are probably hearing this quick rick mantra everywhere "We should be buying foreclosures."

Especially in today's economy, it is difficult to watch the news on television, read a newspaper or magazine without being aware of the massive, current foreclosure problem. Politicians were exploiting these foreclosure woes by campaigning on the basis of a solution to this growing problem to win elections. What a mess!

Reading the next chapter will help you understand why purchasing real estate from the recently departed or from the elderly who are no longer in need of it, is a far better solution than buying foreclosures.

REVIEW OF THE SIX DISADVANTAGES:

- Condition
- Vandalism
- "Insiders"
- Bid Process
- Financing
- Liens, Delinquent Taxes, Second Mortgages

FIVE ADVANTAGES OF "BUYING HOUSES FROM DEAD PEOPLE"

"When you're dead, you're dead. That's it."

Marlene Dietrich

Now that you are aware and know the six key disadvantages of buying foreclosures, let's get into why "Buy Houses From Dead People" has a better solution. First, I hope you understand that you are not really buying from dead people. You will be buying homes from lawyers, family members and/or executors of estates or maybe an elderly person who is:

- Downsizing into an apartment.
- Moving in with their children because the responsibility of maintaining their home is too much.
- Relocating to assisted-living.

The reason really doesn't matter. The fact is that they no longer need their homes and you can buy them. Listed below are some of the advantages to you, the buyer, when purchasing these available homes:

ADVANTAGE #1 - MORTGAGE FREE

If the person no longer in need of their property is elderly, chances are that their mortgage has been paid in full for years. I'm talking thirty or forty years! Think of the appreciation on the original purchase price. These houses don't have second mortgages, delinquent taxes or liens on them. They are free and clear of any debt. A paid for property with no other debt is the perfect example of what you should be looking for because the owner can literally "cash out."

My experience has proven to me more than not that most elderly people care for their homes. They spend money on maintaining or even upgrading their systems. Furnaces, air conditioners, wells, septic systems and roofs are usually in good working condition. You may even find that the homeowner has replaced some of these systems with the top-of-the-line products, because after all, their home's mortgage has been paid in full for years enabling them to invest a little more.

ADVANTAGE #2 - NO REALTOR FEES

If you do your homework and research potential properties in advance and act without hesitation, you should be able to seal the deal without a realtor. Ouch! The realtors will not like the sound of that. I don't want to begrudge them a living, but I am trying to get a deal. No realtor fees will save the seller 6% to 7%. Yes, the seller typically pays the realtor fees, but we all know who really does…it's you, the buyer. Eliminating realtor fees will be perceived by the seller as value added by putting additional cash in his pocket.

ADVANTAGE #3 - NO COMPETITION

Competition is usually non-existent. Why? Because you contact the family members of the recently departed or you contact the elderly person who wants to sell his home **before** the property is available or on the real estate market. Your purchase of this real estate will be "closed" before anyone even realizes it was for sale. Elimination of competition gives you that extra little time (24 hours) to make a wise decision based on **facts** of condition, not **feelings** of competitiveness.

ADVANTAGE #4 - MULTIPLE FAMILY MEMBERS

Earlier, I suggested that houses you "Buy From Dead People" could be purchased for as low as 65% of their current market value. One of the key factors to getting a great deal is **multiple family members**, especially if they live out of town. Why? You ask. The reason is because the money will be divided amongst them.

Let's say you are purchasing a property from an estate. The proceeds will be divided between five relatives. Think about this. The property is worth $300,000. Divide that amount by five heirs and that equals $60,000 each. If you offer $200,000 (two-thirds of the asking price) the proceeds change to $40,000 each. Not a noticeable difference.

Some might say that this **is** a noticeable difference. However, when you add back in the savings of $18,000 (6%) in realtor fees, not to mention time and travel costs, the margin narrows.

Keep in mind, that when dealing with multiple family members, that a fast transaction is often an important factor. Fast is important to the family members, otherwise they will have to pay out of "their" pockets:
- Taxes
- Utilities
- Insurance
- Realtor fees
- Lawn service
- Travel expenses
- Time off work
- Other maintenance expenses

Who is going to be in charge of maintaining the property? This is where the, "they live out of town" factor comes in. They have their own lives to live. They may not be excited about your offer, but chances are that they will take it for the convenience of time and out of pocket money expenditures.

ADVANTAGE # 5 - DATED DÉCOR

This is the fun part. Dated décor can make a home look tired, dull and downright dreary leaving the owner or family members under the impression that its value is much less.

Let's get those heavy gold drapes off the windows and let some light in! Unless the elderly person whose house you are purchasing was really current or you really love avocado green sculptured carpeting…it's going to need redecorating. I said redecorating, not remodeling, there is a big difference.

Redecorating is updating:
- Paint
- Carpet
- Countertops
- Cabinets
- Faucets
- Light fixtures

Remodeling is repairing or replacing:
- Plumbing
- Heating/air conditioning
- Roofs/gutters/siding/etc.
- Drywall/doors/woodwork
- Complete kitchen
- Complete bathroom/rooms

Please understand the differences as they can alter the purchasing process.

Redecorating is fun and can be inexpensive if you are a creative and savvy buyer. Remodeling can be expensive, dirty, time consuming and just downright hard work. How much fun can replacing a furnace be? A new furnace looks the same as the old one. Okay, it's a little smaller and it's beige instead of gray. Maybe it is a girl thing not to appreciate the looks of a new furnace, but a fresh coat of paint on the walls, in a great new color with complimentary trim and new carpeting on the floor…Wow! "It pops!" as my designer would say.

Mortgage free, well maintained but dated décor properties should be your purchasing goal. Multiple family members and the elimination of a realtor are the icing on the cake. This all sounds good, but how do you find these opportunities?

REVIEW OF ADVANTAGES

- Mortgage Free
- No Realtor Fees
- No Competition
- Multiple Family Members
- Dated Décor

CHOOSING A NEIGHBORHOOD

*"Before anything else,
preparation is the key to success."*

Alexander Graham Bell

Picking out your neighborhood in advance is important to good decision making when purchasing a house. Every book and realtor will tell you the three most important words in real estate are "<u>LOCATION, LOCATION, LOCATION.</u>" Don't forget them!

Even in the heat of passion when you love the house and think you have to have it. Even if the sellers are "giving it away!" If it is not in a good location, no matter how great the house may be, even if it is unbelievably cheap and your heart is saying "Yes! Yes! Yes!" your mind should be saying "No! No! No!" **Don't buy it!** The neighborhood will greatly impact your happiness and projected profit.

My first recommendation is to purchase a map of the county in which you want to purchase a house or where you want to live. Circle the areas that are most desirable to you. Drive through the neighborhoods or down the county roads.

Become familiar with the areas.
- Are the streets and roads well kept?
- How about the houses?
- Are they in need of repair or in good condition?
- How do the yards look?
- Are they well manicured?
- Any junk like; cars, boats, old motor homes, trailers?
- Listen. Is it quiet or noisy?

All of these could affect your profit.

Don't drive by an area just once. Hang out. Drive by at different times of the day. Go as often as you can. How does the school district rate? Schools can increase, as well as decrease, property values. Really get to know "all" the aspects of the area.

Let's get more specific by digging into the heart of these properties. Houses in foreclosure are often vacant and in need of repair because the homeowners ran out of the adequate funds needed to maintain their real estate. Frequently, these homeowners will also lose interest in working on their property. They realize that the end is near, their foreclosure papers are on the way and they will soon be forced to move. This may not always be factual, but from my experience, it is true in most cases.

As a potential buyer, you need to look for things like:
- Broken windows
- Ripped screens

- Bad paint
- Overgrown bushes
- Unsightly lawn

Look a little closer. Do you see:
- Old newspapers on the ground?
- Mail accumulating in the mail box?
- Pink or yellow notices on the door?

Ouch! Who wants that? If you can see that on the outside, you can only just imagine what the inside must look like. There is little to no money available for upkeep or maintenance on the property. My guess is the owners probably owe more on their mortgage than the house is worth.

Now, let's seek out a house of an elderly person. First, the mailbox is old and made of metal, mounted on a steel pipe at the end of the driveway. From all appearances the mailbox looks like it has been out there for 100 years. Younger homeowners replace these mailboxes with ones made of rugged, rust-proof plastic.

Now, notice the front screen/storm door. If it is the old style, white or maybe unpainted aluminum with a small window, you are on the right track. Again, younger homeowners tend to replace these old doors with new full glass/screen doors painted to match the color of their house, achieving greater curb appeal.

Are the bushes large and overgrown but look like they have always been maintained? How about that garage door? Is it the old wooden type with windows across the middle or a new metal panel door? Observe the home's windows. Do they look like they have the old style curtains? You can recognize them. They are dreary old shears with heavy drapes on traverse rods. Are you starting to get the picture?

Let's get more specific. This is when I almost feel like a stalker because I am evaluating every element of the property. Does the car in the driveway have Florida license plates? In the winter, is the driveway plowed or does it look like no one lives there? Overall, does the house look well maintained but is just a little tired? It probably belongs to someone who is elderly and has lived there for years. And yes…the mortgage was paid in full years ago.

Take a drive and see what you can observe.

You think you have spotted the house of an elderly person and you are excited. We need to get back to evaluating the neighborhood. The house you have your eye on appeals to you…but what about the houses surrounding it?

Let's review the previous list.
- Are the streets and roads well kept?
- How about the surrounding houses?
- Are they in need of repair or in good condition?
- How do the yards look?
- Are they well manicured?
- Is there any junk; cars, boats, old motor homes, trailers?
- Listen. Is it noisy or quiet?

Also, look around for foreclosed property. You do not want to own property in a neighborhood dotted with foreclosures. Foreclosed properties are not only unsightly, but will reduce the value of the properties surrounding them.

It has often been stated that, "You want to purchase the smallest and lowest priced house in a neighborhood, instead of the largest and most expensive house in a neighborhood."

Stop for a moment and really think about that statement. Why would you want the smallest and the most inexpensive house in a neighborhood? The reason is because the value of the house will automatically be increased by the value of the surrounding properties being higher. On the other side of the coin, the value of the most expensive house in a neighborhood will automatically be decreased by the value of the surrounding properties being lower.

Please read the previous two paragraphs again and completely understand their relevance.

Choosing a profitable neighborhood and understanding the differences between a foreclosure and a mortgage free piece of real estate, are the key essentials to your profitability.

The next chapter will further explore why you must fully understand the values of your neighborhood.

KNOWING NEIGHBORHOOD PROPERTY VALUES

"Luck is what happens when preparation meets opportunity."

Darrell Royal

You have chosen the neighborhoods that you have deemed acceptable for owning property. The next step is to start researching the current market values of the real estate in those neighborhoods.

Read the real estate ads in the local newspaper. Notice that the homes just recently listed are featured with a nice size ad and picture announcing them as a new listing on the real estate market. Also pictured are the homes that have been on the market for a long length of time and their real estate listings are close to expiring. This is done to regenerate interest in the property before the real estate agent loses the listing.

Stop by local hotels and restaurants and pick up the free "Houses for Sale" magazines you see in their lobbies.

Another source of information is "For Sale by Owner" property.

Familiarize yourself with the:
- Asking price
- Selling price
- Turnover of homes
- Condition
- Number of days on the market

Have fun with this. You will be surprised how quickly you can become acquainted with real estate.

You will soon gain the knowledge of:
- Property that sold for a steal
- Property that is priced too high
- Property that will sell quickly
- Property that generated top dollar

Another source of valuable information is to drive around neighborhoods and talk to neighbors out mowing their lawns. People are usually friendly and more than happy to give you information on the area.

While you are having a friendly chat, ask them:
- The amount of time they have lived in the neighborhood?
- If they enjoy living there?
- How many houses are rentals?
- Would they recommend the neighborhood to their friends?

- Are their neighbors friendly?
- What is the average age of the people who live in the neighborhood?
- If there is a large turnover in ownership?
- Do they know of any houses that may be coming up for sale?

Your goal is to gather as much information regarding the area as possible. This information may not seem important to you at this time. You will have to believe me when I say that when the time comes and you are faced with making a quick purchasing decision (good deals do not last long), you will recall this information and it will be invaluable.

As I have stated before, become informed about the school district in the neighborhood.
- What is the school district?
- How close is the grade school, junior high and high school?
- How old are the school buildings?
- Do the children walk or ride the bus?
- Where is the bus stop?
- What is the average class room size of students?
- What is the graduation rate of the high school?
- What is the college acceptance rate after high school?

You may not see the relevance of these school questions if you do not have school children. Do not make the costly mistake by missing the point. A good school district will bring in extra dollars when it is time to sell, just as a poor school district will lower the price.

It has been my experience that most real estate agencies have Multiple Listing Service (MLS) magazines outside their offices available to you at no charge. MLS magazines feature properties from several different real estate agencies. These can provide you with a wealth of knowledge.

Talk to realtors. Go into their sales offices and look at the homes they have listed and have recently sold displayed on their sales board.

Ask these real estate sales professionals:
- How the market is performing?
- The sale's dollar amount below (or sometimes above) the listing price?
- What is the average time the properties located in your neighborhood of interest are on the market before they are sold?

You may feel guilty about gathering information from realtors because you do not intend to purchase from them at this time. Let that feeling go. Sometime in the future you may be in need of their services. You can also return the favor by referring them to your friends and acquaintances. Who knows, they may even direct you to a good deal.

Don't forget the strong impact foreclosures can have on neighborhood's property values. Even the strongest of neighborhoods can be affected by trashed or vandalized foreclosures, sold for unbelievable rock bottom prices. These properties lower the area's "comps" (comparables), thereby reducing the mortgage amount that a bank is willing to lend.

An important factor in your property's appraisal is the selling price and condition of the other properties surrounding yours. Remember what I stated previously about owning the least expensive house in a neighborhood? Banks lend on a mortgage based on a property's appraisal. Appraisals are based on surrounding properties.

Gather all the information you can to determine the area's current market values. You need to know this information to make an informed and accurate offer when it comes your time to make an offer to purchase. How else will you know if you are getting a good deal for a greater profit when you sell it?

EVALUATING YOUR ABILITIES

"The meeting of preparation with opportunity generates the offspring we call luck."

Tony Robbins

So you think you're handy and you have great taste. "You betcha!" to quote Sarah Palin. Maybe so. Who am I to judge? After all, I believed that I was the queen of decorating just because I could get a room or two looking pretty decent. I am good, but my designer is superior. This is important and I will tell you why in a later chapter.

For now, let's get back to being "handy." Can you:
- Climb a ladder and tuck point the chimney?
- Remove the old roof and install a new roof straight and without leaks?
- Dispose of that old roof? That can be costly.
- Scrape, paint or install vinyl siding on the exterior of the house?
- Replace that front door?
- Install a new garage door?

- Replace the mailbox?
- Dig out and replace the bushes improving the curb appeal?
- Coordinate paint, carpet, countertops and fixtures like a designer?

If you can't perform these tasks and you cannot recuperate the costs by hiring someone else…**Don't buy a house that needs these repairs!**

Do you possess the skills of a:
- Plumber?
- Electrician?
- Carpenter?
- Mason?
- Painter?

Will you have to pay for the deliveries of your materials? This can be an overlooked expense of $25 to $100 for each delivery.

Do you own the proper tools? What amount will you have to spend to purchase the tools you will need to complete the job? This may be an additional expense that needs to be included in your job costs. You may also consider renting tools.

Evaluating your abilities in advance will aid you on your selection of the house you buy. Keep in mind that you may have friends and family who can help you. But remember that there is "no free lunch" when it comes to free help. You will have to pay it back…it's your obligation! You may not directly pay back the person who helped you. It may be someone else, at a later date and time, after you have acquired some skills, but it is your duty.

Ask yourself the following questions. Be brutally honest with yourself.
- Will you be able to do the work yourself?
- Do you possess the skills?
- Will you have to hire the work done?
- Will your friends and family **really** be available to help you?
- Will you have the time required to complete the work?

Do not make the mistake of taking on more than you can handle.

There are an abundance of "How To" books and "Do It Yourself" programs on television. These resources can fool you. The projects look so easy when the work is completed in these books and on these programs. What you don't see are the large crews with the best tools stepping in (during the commercials) completing the work. The workers never seem to run into any obstacles or problems. The jobs the crews are working on always seem to be perfectly level. The materials they are using always match the old materials and the workers never cut anything wrong. The job always goes smoothly, without a hitch. Reality? I don't think so.

Kidding yourself on your abilities can be a big and costly mistake. When you are working weekday evenings, Saturdays and Sundays by yourself with no one available to hold the "idiot end," you will be wondering, "What the heck did I do!?!" (No one said making money or making things better for yourself would be easy.)

So eliminate all distractions and sit in a quiet place. Take your time and evaluate your specific skills as noted on the following "Assessing Your Abilities" worksheets. Upon completion, ask your wife, husband or a good friend to look them over and see if they agree with your self-assessment. If **they** say **you** can do it, make sure **they** will do the work, if **you** really can't.

EVALUATING YOUR ABILITIES WORKSHEETS

"Management by objectives
works if you first think through your objectives.
Ninety percent of the time you haven't."

Peter Drucker

WORKSHEET A

TASK	Y	N	W/HELP	HIRE	NOTES
Remove/replace roof					
Repair/replace gutters					
Scrape/paint exterior					
Install vinyl siding					
Replace exterior doors					
Install new mailbox					
Replace garage door					
Repair broken windows					

WORKSHEET B

TASK	Y	N	W/HELP	HIRE	NOTES
Remove/dispose old landscape					
Design/install new landscape					
Remove/replace sidewalks/drive					
Repair/replace fencing					
Remove old carpeting					
Sand/refinish hardwood floors					
Replace faucets/vanities					
Repair/replace ceramic tile					

WORKSHEET C

TASK	Y	N	W/HELP	HIRE	NOTES
Replace toilet/repair floor					
Replace light fixtures					
Repair drywall/plaster					
Replace garage door					
Paint/prepare walls					
Replace kitchen cabinets					
Replace countertops					
Replace furnace/air conditioner					

WORKSHEET D

TASK	Y	N	W/HELP	HIRE	NOTES
Replace hot water heater					
Repair foundation problems					
Repair fireplace					
Repair/replace plumbing					
Repair/replace electrical					

KNOWING YOUR COSTS

---

*"If we knew what it was we were doing,
it would not be called research, would it?"*

Albert Einstein

Buying a house in need of repair, fixing it up and selling it for a profit appears simple and easy. It can be. I preach everyday that it is. And it **is** simple and easy…for me, but many people struggle. Their projects fail to be profitable because they jumped into decisions without proper preparation.

Projects fall flat due to the lack of planning. People make the enormous mistake of purchasing a house without adequate knowledge of costs related to the repairs and upgrades.

By "costs," I mean the price of material and labor. The <u>true</u> price of material and labor, not a guess, not what you think they should be, not what your brother-in-law says they are, but an exact, accurate knowledge of material and labor costs in your area.

Knowing the total cost of a repair or upgrade in advance will aid you in avoiding the accumulation of unanticipated expenses that consume your profits. This is the information that makes buying and selling for a profit simple and easy. Hear these words and remember them…**know your costs!**

Just think of the warm fuzzy feeling you can get when you walk into a prospective house in need of new appliances and know the amount of money that those appliances are going to set you back.

Or that new roof it's going to need and thinking "Yes, it will look great!" The new roof is worth the upgrade because you know exactly what it is going to cost.

Refinish those hardwood floors in need of a good sanding and refinishing? You know the exact cost per square foot and what a bang for the buck!

Does the house have a shabby looking front door? Not a problem, because you know where to go to buy that great new door and that it will only cost you a couple of hundred dollars.

You will have all this security and self assurance because you did your homework. There are no surprises in your future.

Keep in mind, when you are setting up and analyzing your costs that there are levels of housing grades.

LOW-LEVEL HOUSE

You may call a small, simple and low priced house…a low-level house. Maybe you are planning on making it a rental.

Using hollow doors, minimal woodwork, inexpensive cabinets, hardware and fixtures would be adequate. As far as the labor is concerned, a handyman is the skill level of carpentry that would serve your needs.

MID-LEVEL HOUSE

What about a mid-level house? If you purchased this house to "flip," or for yourself and your family to live in, I want to recommend that you use materials that have a minimum quality of mid-grade to lower high-end on almost everything. Install six panel solid wood doors. Spend the additional 10% to buy stainless steel appliances instead of white. If the countertops do not require too many square feet, you may want to go ahead and splurge on granite.

Let me explain why. Even though the house is mid-level, upgrading it with higher quality products will create a perception of a higher level of house. This is important in achieving a greater profit in flipping or creating a higher standard of living for yourself and your family.

If you buy cheap products, you achieve a cheap perception and you will get cheap offers. I know you may feel like a higher expense is additional money out of your pocket, but I believe you will enjoy a greater return on your investment. Oh, one more thing…hire a good carpenter for good finish work.

HIGH-LEVEL HOUSE

You have just purchased a high-end luxury home in an exclusive neighborhood on the ocean for a steal. Great! Pat yourself on the back. Now, let's make some money.

You've completed your homework and you know the price of the new Sub Zero refrigerator the kitchen is going to need. You have checked out the prices of repairing a sprinkler system, so you will have no surprises there.

Be careful. Missing an item or not knowing your costs of material and labor on a high-end luxury home can diminish your profits fast.

Have you ever replaced a slate or tile roof? What about repairing a stucco exterior? Do you know how much a master finish carpenter or mason charges per hour?

This house needs a new shower that is not only functional... but **fabulous**, with multiple showerheads and a built-in stereo system. (You've seen them on TV...right?) You had better be thinking high-end or custom on everything. I see the money flowing out of your pockets already.

High-end can mean higher risk and that can equal higher profit. Know what you are doing and what repairs or upgrades the property is going to need. Figure out your costs and what you are going to spend before you purchase this level of real estate and you will make the correct decision. If you feel the profit will not be equal or greater than the amount of work and investment, walk away and find another opportunity. Again, for your sake, I say...**know your costs!**

ASSEMBLING YOUR TEAM

"Talent wins games,
but teamwork and intelligence
wins championships."

Michael Jordan

Working with a team that you pre-selected will help you accomplish your goals. Your team should include a:

- Banker
- Lawyer
- House Inspector
- Surveyor
- Designer/Decorator
- Your "Gut"

Going it alone or thinking you can do it all yourself is foolish. From my experience and results, I firmly believe that the expertise of the following six professionals will more than pay for themselves. Let's examine the need and duties of these six team members.

TEAM MEMBER #1 - BANKER

If you have a long time relationship with a banker you are ahead of the game. They know your credit history, financial position and possibly your financial goals.

If you currently do not have a relationship with a bank professional, you need to obtain one. Find a banker that you feel will work hard for you and get them quickly up to speed on your goals and on how you are planning to achieve them.

If your bank professional seems skeptical about your methods…find a different banker! Remember, bankers can be "insiders" and realtors are their friends. They may feel uncomfortable cutting their friends out of the money making pie. The banker may also feel that buying real estate directly from a seller without a realtor will cause them to do additional work. Assure your banker that your lawyer will be coordinating the paperwork with them. Establish your limits with their bank and have them pre-approve your financing.

TEAM MEMBER #2 - LAWYER

The same goes for your lawyer as with your banker. If you have a relationship with one, that is great.

You don't need an expensive, big name lawyer. This is a real estate deal, not a murder case. It's just paperwork. Paperwork that is important, accurate and in your best interest because once signed, it becomes a **legal** and **binding** contract.

You need to hire an attorney that will do his due diligence and understand your need for speed. Explain your methods of obtaining property and why his availability and quick response time is important and required.

It is not necessary to pay an arm and a leg for these services. Establish a fair hourly rate. Consider that your lawyer and his staff's duties may include:
- Gathering information from the courthouse
- Drawing up an "Offer to Purchase" agreement
- Ordering title work
- Reviewing the deed and loan contracts
- Attending the closing

All this work you can do yourself, but I advise against it. A lawyer's fee will look like pennies compared to a lawsuit.

TEAM MEMBER #3 - HOUSE INSPECTOR

Your **"right to cancel"** after the house inspection within 48 hours after acceptance of your offer, is the one and only chance you have to back out of the deal. Back out only if your inspector finds a major problem. By a major problem, I mean something that would be difficult or expensive to repair. Discovering contaminated soil or extensive termite damage could be causes for voiding the contract.

Make sure your inspector is certified, qualified and thorough. Remember that you are buying the property "as is." (A disclosure statement from the seller is not required by the state if the property is in an estate.)

Because the person selling the property never owned it, they would be unaware of its current condition. It is you and your house inspector's responsibility to discover any problems.

This is an important point because after the 48 hour inspection time expires, you have no cancellation rights. Remember to ask for references **before** hiring an inspector.

TEAM MEMBER #4 - SURVEYOR

Have the property that you are about to purchased surveyed. You may think that a survey is unnecessary. You may be tempted to skip this step, especially if your bank does not require it, to save money. **Don't!** Your surveyor will define the boundaries. You need to know in advance the location of the property lines and if any encroachments exist.

TEAM MEMBER #5 - DESIGNER

If you are going to be flipping this house for a profit, hire a proven and professional designer/decorator. Have him coordinate:
- Paint
- Wall coverings
- Flooring
- Countertops
- Hardware

I know that you think you have good taste and a good eye for color, but your taste may not be suitable to the general public. You could go all beige or some other neutral color…how boring! Designer/decorators make the world a beautiful place by being current and up-to-date on colors and materials. When a potential buyer walks through the door for the first time, you want the room to "pop!" There is only one chance to make that first impression. Make sure that impression excites your buyer, enticing them to see more.

Your purpose is to acquire as many interested buyers, **with offers**, as possible. It is my experience that for every $500 you spend on a designer, $5000 will be your return. No kidding! The really great thing is that as you purchase more properties, you can replicate the same colors and materials, house to house, without the additional expense of a designer, thereby increasing your returns.

If you are not convinced, just visit several model home open houses. Everything looks so perfect. You feel like you could live there…like you're "home." Do you think that you got that warm, comfortable feeling by accident? Think again!

That model home was **designed** to make you feel that way. It was **designed** to make you want to buy it. I can sense the smell of home baked cookies from here. Yes, they do that too. If your designer is good, he will touch on all senses. Convey your goal and budget when choosing a designer to work with you and they will prove to be invaluable.

TEAM MEMBER #6 - GUT

Your "gut" is probably your most important team member. It is the heart and soul of your property venture. Your "gut" is the heart and soul because it is your "gut," not your banker, lawyer, house inspector, surveyor or designer/ decorator that will bear the wrath of a failed project.

Wraths, for example:
- Loss capital
- Low return on investment
- Loss of time
- Loss of self esteem
- Feelings of failure
- Debt

Reach down into your "gut" when making decisions. Listen to your "gut" above all emotions. Take your "gut" feeling above all advice and opinions from other people. Act on your "gut," even above the advice and opinions of your own team members. If your banker says you **"can"** afford it, but your "gut" says you **"can't"**…don't! When your surveyor says you **"can"** correct the encroachment <u>after</u> you purchase the property, but your "gut" says, **"I don't think so!"**…believe it! Use good judgment. That's what your "gut" is for. So use it!

That's it. Your team is assembled and together you will accomplish great things. Only eliminate a team member if you feel you have the expertise or know someone who has it and will do it for you.

LOCATING AVAILABLE PROPERTIES

---

*"The person who goes the farthest
is generally the one who is willing to
do and dare."*

Dale Carnegie

It's time to start searching for available properties in the neighborhoods you have chosen. There are many avenues you can take.

I suggest that you use as many ways as you can come up with and be **bold** enough to use them. By **"bold"** I mean… Are you willing to volunteer at the hospital or be a volunteer at a nursing home? That would be bold. How about delivering Meals on Wheels?

My sister and brother-in-law wanted to purchase a condo in a very popular complex which rarely has units available. They put their name on a waiting list and figured that it could take a year or two to receive a call.

She learned that a widowed man who owned a condo unit was recently admitted into the hospital and that he most likely would not be returning to his home. My sister and her husband visited this owner in the hospital where they were introduced by his neighbor.

She explained to him that they were having difficulty finding an available condo in his complex and asked if he wanted to sell his unit. He named his selling price, they agreed and wrote up the Offer to Purchase agreement. The owner accepted it, signed it and died three days later. I was so proud of her. They live there now and they love it.

Sounds a little morbid? I can see why you think that, but like I have said, "you are creating a circumstance that benefits two parties while providing a service." My sister created an opportunity to get a fast, good deal on their condo and the family of the deceased has one item off their plate.

Talk the talk to your friends and neighbors. As I wrote earlier, you can secure information from people working out in their yards in the neighborhoods that interest you. Remember to be friendly, not pushy.

Some people are very private and suspicious. They may think you are trying to get information so that you can break into their house in the middle of the night or when they are not at home and rob them. Introduce yourself. Tell them your name and where you live and work. Maybe you have common friends. Tell them you are looking for a home to purchase and admire their neighborhood.

People love to help people. Ask them:
- If they know of a property coming up for sale?
- If they will help you?
- If they will accept your phone number?
- If they will call you if they learn of an available property?

Just by looking neat, clean and presentable you will be surprised at the reactions you receive.

Are you a member of any clubs? Spread the word about your interest in finding a soon to be available property. How about golf or tennis, do you play? Are you a jogger? Do you attend church? Start asking questions.

Take advantage of every situation you can!

Another strategy is using the obituaries listed in the local newspaper, provided that you know what to look for. I want to share with you how I use them.

Let's look at the following example of an obituary:

DOE, JOHN A.

John A. Doe, age 56, longtime Gutterville resident died peacefully on Friday at his home after a long illness with his loving wife of 25 years by his side. He is survived by his wife, Mary and one son, John Jr. also of Gutterville. Services will be held on Monday at the Gutterville funeral home.

I read this obituary and dismissed it right away for many reasons. See if you can figure out why.

First of all, John A Doe was only 56 years old. Chances are that his house is not paid for and may have a second mortgage. He also is survived by his wife who will still need a place to live. And, I hope you see the obvious, that it is located in Gutterville. No one wants to live there. Not a good choice for buying a house to sell for a profit. You will not want to move your family there. Remember what I told you about location?

Here is another one:

SMITH, MARY K.

Mary K. Smith, age 91, lived at 555 Sparkling Waters Lane, Pleasantville, North Carolina. Her husband Sterling preceded her in death. Mrs. Smith is survived by six daughters; Deborah of Indiana, Pat of Illinois, Paula of Nevada, Jane of California, Barbara and Rose both of Ohio.

This could be the jackpot. Do you see why? Mrs. Smith was 91 years of age. Her house was paid for years ago. There is no second mortgage and her husband preceded her in death leaving a vacant house.

Look at the neighborhood. It's a perfect location. You can picture yourself and your spouse raising a family there. Your neighbors will be friendly, with children to play with yours. The house looks a little tired, but with a little paint, some new shrubbery and a little hard work, it will look great!

If the local newspaper does not supply the street address of the deceased, just look in the phone book. It will be listed under Mary K. Smith, MK Smith, M Smith, or Sterling

Smith. You can also go on line to sites that provide addresses as a service.

This property is the jackpot because there are six children, all of whom live in other states. Who's going to take care of the property? When you present them with a low offer, the money will be divided six ways reducing the amount to each by very little.

Understand this point. If you offer $120,000 less than the current market value of the house, that is only $20,000 less to each survivor. But if this was an offer to only one survivor, it would be the full $120,000 deduction to them. That single survivor would be likely to walk away, willing to wait for a higher offer.

One more:

BROWN, BEATRICE B.

Beatrice B. Brown, age 75, of Green Acres, California. She is survived by her husband Dr. Bernard Brown. Mrs. Brown was a retired attorney practicing in the Green Acres area for over 35 years. Beatrice is also survived by 2 daughters, Lauren and Lindsey both of Green Acres, California, 4 grandchildren Michael, Stephen, Joseph and Claire also of Green Aces, California. Funeral services will be held on Saturday at 11:30.

Upon close examination, you will notice that Beatrice was 75 years old and she was an attorney, survived by a husband who is a doctor. They were probably very prosperous and affluent.

Within one month, the old gals around town will be lining up at this widower's front door with casseroles to catch this new single and very available doctor. He doesn't have a chance. Yes, his wife just recently died, but she is dead and gone…what is he to do?

My point is that he will not be alone for very long. One of those ladies will snatch him up fast. He will no longer need his house and it will soon be up for sale. Think I'm wrong? Possibly.

Okay, let's say he is just a not so healthy old man. He's not rich and not even that attractive. Both his daughters are married and successful and own houses that have great live-in guest rooms. These daughters may even have guest houses. They hate to see dad living alone. After all, mom always took such good care of him. Dad could hire help, but his daughters promised mom that they would care for him after she was gone. They will insist that dad will come and live with them and because he is so lonely and in poor health, he probably will. Keep your eye on this one. This house will be up for sale within one year.

Enough of my imaginary obituaries. Now you must start reading and honing your skills on finding clues that help you locate soon to be available properties. Do remember that obituaries are also listed by funeral homes on their web sites if you do not subscribe to the local newspaper. Deaths are also public record. You may want to visit your county courthouse to see what form that information is available to you.

Reading obituaries provide a daily source of possible available properties. From my experience, I feel using this strategy is very important. I want to review these four clues to look for when reading an obituary.

CLUE #1

NAME: Is the deceased male or female? Females tend to live alone better than males. A female survivor will likely live in her current home after her husband's death. Males tend to move.

CLUE #2

AGE: If the deceased was under 60 years of age, it is likely that there is a mortgage and even a second mortgage on their home. You want to find a property with a **"paid in full"** mortgage for your best deal.

CLUE #3

ADDRESS: These are the three most important factors when evaluating the address; LOCATION, LOCATON, LOCATION. If the deceased did not live in the very best location…please move on.

CLUE #4

SURVIVORS: The more survivors listed the better. The money from the sale of the property of the deceased will be divided amongst them. Even better is if the survivors live in a town over an hour away or out of state. No one wants to drive that far to maintain a property and no one certainly wants to pay out of their share to have it done. The older the deceased, the older their children tend to be. Older survivors often want a quick closure to their parent's estate.

Use these four clues to find an even better situation for obtaining a great deal on a piece of real estate and go write the letter outlined in the next chapter.

WRITING THE LETTER

*"Look for your choices, pick the best one,
then go with it."*

Pat Riley

Your research is complete. You have located a piece of real estate that you are interested in pursuing. Now is the time to write the letter.

I'll bet you are feeling a little funny about this, especially if it involves a death. Even after writing numerous letters, I still feel that way too.

Remember the story I shared with you in the first chapter about the great house I lost because I did not want to look like an ambulance chaser? It still hurts. I so much wanted to live in that neighborhood.

Don't hesitate and let an opportunity slip away. Try to remember that you are providing a service.

If a family member does not want the house, it will come up for sale. Someone will have to buy it sooner or later. You are just trying to create a situation that is beneficial to all parties.

It benefits you by being able to purchase it at a lower price. Again, it benefits the seller or estate by providing a quick and effortless sell.

You must ask for the opportunity first by writing the letter. This letter is simple, to the point and has only three parts.

PART #1 - ADDRESSING THE LETTER

If you know the exact name of the person responsible for the sale of the targeted real estate, address it to; Dear_____(insert their name). If you do not have the responsible party's name, address it; To Whom It May Concern or Dear Sir or Madam, whichever you prefer.

PART #2 - BODY OF THE LETTER

Be direct and brief. State your intention and your contact information. Such as; It is my understanding that this house may be for sale. I am interested in purchasing it as is. You can contact me at _____(insert your phone number).

PART #3 - SALUTATION OF THE LETTER

Conclude your letter with; Sincerely or Regards, it is really your preference, along with your name and address. Your name and address are important. They will see that you are not a realtor or someone who is trying to sell them something. They may feel like someone is trying to scam them and this provides the potential seller with information to research you to confirm your intentions. Providing your name and address shows that you are open and writing in good faith.

REVIEW:

Your letter should look something like this:

December 5, XXXX

Dear Sir or Madam,

It is my understanding that this house at (insert the address) may be for sale. I may be interested in purchasing it <u>as is</u>.

You can contact me at (your phone number).

Sincerely,

(Your name)
(Your street address)
(Your City, State and Zip Code)

Writing this letter is simple enough. Sign it and make a copy for your records.

Address an envelope to the address of the property you wish to purchase. Someone is receiving and tending to the mail being sent to this address. Stick a stamp on it and mail it.

You are done. There is nothing more you can do now. Don't stop looking for other properties because the potential sellers may not be interested in pursuing your request and will not contact you. Keep your options open by creating additional opportunities. Do not get discouraged…the right property will come your way.

ASSESSING THE CONDITION

"Experience taught me a few things. One is to listen to your gut, no matter how good something sounds on paper. The second is that you're generally better off sticking with what you know. And the third is that sometimes your best investments are the ones you don't make."

Donald Trump

Your letter has been received and the selling party has called and is interested in talking to you. What's next? Well, you have to make an appointment to look at the property. You know the neighborhood. You've seen the outside. It's time to look inside…and **be ready!** Ready for what?

After you walk through the house be ready to make an offer. No, you can't come back and bring your friends to take a look. You can't even think about making an offer for a few days. **This is a business deal!**

Take everyone who influences your decision with you the first and only time you go inside before making your offer. You will be purchasing this property in "<u>as is</u>" condition.

Be sure you know your scope of work and costs before making an offer. Use the following "Assessing the Condition" worksheets to thoroughly assess the house's need of repairs or upgrades. While you are there, take all the time you need to fill out the "Assessing the Condition" worksheets, room by room, inside and out.

Then go home, total up the "costs" categories and make your decision. You need to be thorough and quick. Remember, time is important in getting a great deal. This needs to be painless for the seller, especially if you want to avoid realtor involvement.

Don't forget that you have included in your offer the right to an inspection up to 48 hours after your offer to purchase has been accepted. This does give you an out if your inspector finds any surprises.

Is the importance of knowing your neighborhood values, your abilities, your costs on labor and materials, your banker, your lawyer and your inspector starting to sink in? If you do not look like you know what you are doing, an inexperienced seller will be left in fear and doubt of selling their property themselves. You told them that you are interested in buying it…so, are you or not?

You will also be able to use your "Assessing the Condition" worksheets when making your offer to purchase the property by sharing them with the seller. This will show the seller the work and expense of bringing their house up to date. If you are working with an executor, they will be able to use these worksheets as a tool in persuading the other family members to accept your offer, justifying the lower price.

ASSESSING THE
CONDITION WORKSHEETS

---

*"Opportunity is missed by most people
because it is dressed in overalls
and looks like work."*

Thomas A. Edison

WORKSHEET A

GENERAL	OK	REPAIR/REPLACE	MATERIAL COSTS	LABOR COSTS	NOTES
Insulation					
Stairs					
Interior Doors					
Woodwork					
Outlets/Switches					
Well/Septic					
Electrical					
Plumbing					

WORKSHEET B

EXTERIOR	OK	REPAIR/REPLACE	MATERIAL COSTS	LABOR COSTS	NOTES
Foundation					
Roof					
Soffit					
Siding					
Windows					
Doors					
Door Bell					
Garage Door					

WORKSHEET C

EXTERIOR	OK	REPAIR/REPLACE	MATERIAL COSTS	LABOR COSTS	NOTES
Gutters					
Steps					
Sidewalks					
Driveway					
Light Fixtures					
Mailbox					
Landscape					
Grass					

WORKSHEET D

EXTERIOR	OK	REPAIR/REPLACE	MATERIAL COSTS	LABOR COSTS	NOTES
Trees					
Fencing					
Pool					
Sheds					
Chimney					
Vents					
Other					

WORKSHEET E

INTERIOR KITCHEN	OK	REPAIR/REPLACE	MATERIAL COSTS	LABOR COSTS	NOTES
Size					
Walls/Ceiling					
Cabinets/Knobs					
Counter Tops					
Sink/Faucet					
Appliances					
Lighting					
Flooring					

WORKSHEET F

INTERIOR BATHROOM 1	OK	REPAIR/REPLACE	MATERIAL COSTS	LABOR COSTS	NOTES
Size					
Walls/Ceiling					
Vanity/Knobs					
Sink/Faucet					
Bathtub/Shower					
Toilet					
Lighting					
Flooring					

WORKSHEET G

INTERIOR BATHROOM 2	OK	REPAIR/REPLACE	MATERIAL COSTS	LABOR COSTS	NOTES
Size					
Walls/Ceiling					
Vanity/Knobs					
Sink/Faucet					
Bathtub/Shower					
Toilet					
Lighting					
Flooring					

WORKSHEET H

INTERIOR DINING ROOM	OK	REPAIR/REPLACE	MATERIAL COSTS	LABOR COSTS	NOTES
Size					
Walls/Ceiling					
Lighting					
Flooring					
Built-ins					
Other					

WORKSHEET I

INTERIOR LIVING ROOM	OK	REPAIR/REPLACE	MATERIAL COSTS	LABOR COSTS	NOTES
Size					
Walls/Ceiling					
Lighting					
Flooring					
Fireplace					
Built-ins					
Other					

WORKSHEET J

INTERIOR FAMILY ROOM	OK	REPAIR/REPLACE	MATERIAL COSTS	LABOR COSTS	NOTES
Size					
Walls/Ceiling					
Lighting					
Flooring					
Fireplace					
Built-ins					
Other					

WORKSHEET K

INTERIOR OFFICE	OK	REPAIR/REPLACE	MATERIAL COSTS	LABOR COSTS	NOTES
Size					
Walls/Ceiling					
Lighting					
Flooring					
Built-ins					
Other					

WORKSHEET L

INTERIOR BEDROOM 1	OK	REPAIR/REPLACE	MATERIAL COSTS	LABOR COSTS	NOTES
Size					
Walls/Ceiling					
Closets					
Lighting					
Flooring					
Built-ins					
Other					

WORKSHEET M

INTERIOR BEDROOM 2	OK	REPAIR/REPLACE	MATERIAL COSTS	LABOR COSTS	NOTES
Size					
Walls/Ceiling					
Closets					
Lighting					
Flooring					
Built-ins					
Other					

WORKSHEET N

INTERIOR BEDROOM 3	OK	REPAIR/REPLACE	MATERIAL COSTS	LABOR COSTS	NOTES
Size					
Walls/Ceiling					
Closets					
Lighting					
Flooring					
Built-ins					
Other					

WORKSHEET O

INTERIOR LAUNDRY ROOM	OK	REPAIR/REPLACE	MATERIAL COSTS	LABOR COSTS	NOTES
Size					
Walls/Ceiling					
Lighting					
Flooring					
Water Hookup					
Drain					
Electrical (GFI's)					

WORKSHEET P

INTERIOR BASEMENT	OK	REPAIR/REPLACE	MATERIAL COSTS	LABOR COSTS	NOTES
Size					
Walls/Ceiling					
Lighting					
Concrete					
Water Damage					
Furnace					
Air Conditioning					

WORKSHEET Q

INTERIOR BASEMENT	OK	REPAIR/REPLACE	MATERIAL COSTS	LABOR COSTS	NOTES
Water Softner					
Sink/Faucet					
Storage					
Floor Drain					
Fuel Tank					
Electrical Service					
Plumbing					

WORKSHEET R

INTERIOR GARAGE	OK	REPAIR/REPLACE	MATERIAL COSTS	LABOR COSTS	NOTES
Size					
Walls/Ceiling					
Lighting					
Floor Drain					
Water Faucets					
Concrete					
Door Opener					
Storage/Other					

MAKING AN OFFER

"You can have everything in life you want,
if you will just help other people
get what they want."

Zig Zigler

Your homework is complete and the letter you have written was successful. You have viewed the interior of the house along with your designer and you've filled out the "Assessing the Condition" worksheets.

<u>Go home and make a decision!</u> Not tomorrow, not the next day…**now!** You have been driving by this piece of real estate for over a week. You have assessed the land, the exterior of the house and outbuildings…now act! Decide on the price you are willing to pay and call your lawyer. As Nike says, "Just Do It."

Now is the time you find out if you've chosen the right lawyer. Yes, he has to be an attorney who is at your beckon call. He has to act in a quick and thorough manner. He has to be

---

able to produce an Offer to Purchase Agreement within 24 hours. Two to twelve hours would be even better.

Your "Offer to Purchase" agreement should include the following:
- Address of the property
- Legal description of the real estate
- Sellers correct, legal names
- Your correct, legal name
- Your offer should state that you will be purchasing the property "as is" subject to an inspection within 48 hours after acceptance of the offer to purchase.
- Purchase price
- Earnest money down
- Subject to financing
- Agreement expiration date
- Closing expiration date
- Signature lines for Sellers and Buyers
- Signature lines for Witnesses

(Yes, you have been pre-approved, but it is usually subject to the appraisal.)

List any extras to be included such as:
- Appliances
- Window coverings
- Rugs
- Lawn or garden ornaments
- Water softener (often rented)
- Removable sheds
- Etc.

Your lawyer will advise you on additional information based on the circumstances; private owner, in an estate, etc. State the amount and conditions of your earnest money down to secure the offer. All you need now are signature lines for you, the Buyer and for them, the Sellers.

Standard "Offer to Purchase" blank forms are available on line or can be purchased at your local office supplies store. If you choose to go this route and complete the "Offer to Purchase" agreement yourself, I highly recommend you have your attorney review it before making your presen-tation. The "Offer to Purchase" agreement once signed by each party is a legal and binding contract and should be taken very serious. Do not skip your lawyer's review, espe-cially if this is your first time offer.

Your "Offer to Purchase" agreement is complete and you are all set to move forward. Call the sellers and make an appointment to make your offer.

When presenting your offer, take two copies of the "Of-fer to Purchase" agreement signed by you, the Buyer. One is for you and one is for the Seller. Include your earnest money check payable to the Seller. Tell the Seller that you are already approved for financing (on the condition the property meets the selling price) and that you can close as soon as the paperwork necessary for closing is completed. Give them you banker's business card so they can confirm this statement. (Make sure you have given your banker permission to give out this information due to the new privacy laws.) Then leave.

You have done all you can at this point. The decision is in the sellers hands to accept or reject your offer.

Now you have to wait for their response.

CLOSING THE DEAL

"Let us never negotiate out of fear.
But let us never fear to negotiate."

John F. Kennedy

The wait is over. The sellers have accepted your offer. Good for you! You can skip the rest of this chapter and contact your lawyer to order the title work and start coordinating the closing. If your offer was not accepted, please read on.

The owners likely rejected your offer because:
- They feel like they don't know what they are doing.
- They are afraid they will make a legal mistake.
- They feel security in hiring a realtor.
- They think they can get a higher price.

The owners may feel that they do not have the experience or ability to sell a house themselves. Most people only buy or sell one, two or three houses in their lifetime. Many may never experience buying or selling a house at all.

Entering into a legal contract with a stranger can make an owner feel uncomfortable. They may be unfamiliar with the legal real estate terms and are not willing to learn them.

Realtors can be viewed as seasoned professionals. Some are and some…not so much. Realtors are <u>property sales</u> professionals, not <u>legal</u> professionals. Realtor or not, the sellers need to have any contracts reviewed by their attorney. Sellers should remember that realtors work on commission and may influence them for the benefit of themselves. Realtors do not earn commissions on real estate deals made directly between a seller and a buyer.

The sellers may feel they will receive a higher selling price due to the higher exposure a realtor can supply. Higher exposure will take time. As I said before, time takes money and what family member wants that?

Still, many sellers will seek the comfort of a realtor. You are just going to have to wait and deal with their realtor using the same process. Chances are you will still be able to purchase the house for the same low price, but at a later date. The sellers will have to pay the realtor fees for their perceived security and convenience.

If the sellers return to you with a counter offer, you have some decisions to make. You can:
- Accept their counter offer.
- Counter offer their counter offer.
- Reject their counter offer, but extend your original offer to a later date.
- Reject their counter offer, forget the property and start working on your next deal.

Accept their counter offer:

I feel your knees shaking. This is no time to buckle under the pressure. If you cannot agree on a price...**be willing to walk away!**

Counter their counter offer:

If they counter offer your offer, show them your "Assessing the Condition" worksheets pointing out the work that will need to be done to repair or upgrade the property. If you are willing to pay a little more, present your counter offer.

Reject their counter offer, but extend your original offer to a later date:

If you are not willing to up your offer, you could tell them to go ahead, try to sell the property for more money and if they are not successful they can come back to you at a later date. At that later date you will extend your original offer. Again, you can show the sellers the completed "Assessing the Condition" worksheets so they can clearly see the work and improvements their real estate is going to need.

Reject their counter offer, forget the property and start working on your next deal:

Or as always, if you decide that the right decision is to walk away...do so. Shake it off and start over again. You may have become so emotionally involved that letting go is hard to do, but move on. Go find the next great deal.

There will <u>always</u> be a **"NEXT GREAT DEAL"** out there if you are willing to do the work to find it. Walking away may be the key to getting a great deal later, verses just getting an okay deal now.

ARE YOU READY?

*"By failing to prepare,
you are preparing to fail."*

Benjamin Franklin

After you have:
- Located a potential property
- Written and mailed the letter
- Been contacted by the property owner
- Viewed the inside of the house

Are you ready to make the decision of offering to purchase this real estate within twenty-four hours? Your response to the following questions will allow you to make that decision.

24 HOURS TO PURCHASE

CHECKLIST

_____ Do you have your neighborhoods selected?

_____ Do you know your selected neighborhood's property values?

_____Do you know your abilities?

_____Do you know your costs of labor and materials?

_____Do you have your "Assessing the Condition" worksheets?

_____Do you have your Banker?

_____Do you have your Lawyer?

_____Do you have your Inspector?

_____Do you have your Surveyor?

_____Do you have your Designer?

_____Do you have a good feeling in your "Gut?"

If you have checked all of the above, you are ready to go! Now you can pursue purchasing real estate and proceed with confidence because you have done your homework.

Now is not the time to second guess yourself. You've prepared in advance and you will make an informed decision. Now go have some fun!